WHAT DOES SELF-ESTEEM HAVE TO DO WITH CHARACTER?

Mary Porter White

WHAT DOES SELF-ESTEEM HAVE TO DO WITH CHARACTER?

Copyright © 2013 by Mary Porter White
Layout and Design: Tony Bradford

All Scripture quotations, unless otherwise indicated were taken from the Holy Bible, King James Version.

ISBN 978-1-938950-37-7
Greater is He Publishing

9824 E. Washington St. Chagrin Falls, Ohio

44023 P O. Box 46115 Bedford Ohio, 44146

http://www.greaterishepublishing.com

216-288-9315

Dedication

This book is dedicated to both of my beautiful grand-daughters. Both of whom have taught me how wonderful it can be to be a grandmother. Both of whom have given me an opportunity to love each of them individually, and to keep separate places in my heart for each of them. Both have given me opportunities to celebrate their difference in personalities and enjoyments of life.

Although God has blessed both girls with beautiful singing voices; each of them have allowed me to sing along with them while they sang their favorite songs to me as young girls which were "Amazing Grace" and "Good Morning Jesus."

I shall forever cherish my first birthday cake that I still have made out of Styrofoam and painted with water colors by my oldest granddaughter and the making of my first teddy bear with my younger granddaughter still in my possession. Each priceless and precious!

Maat you are a peace maker and so ful of Love!

The eyes of the
Lord are upon you

You are a very special child
whom God has blessed
and given you special gifts!

You will always be my sugar
plum and apple pie!

I have had and do have so much
fun with you; you are a pleasure
to be with — I am so glad you
are my granddaughter

Table of Contents

Appendix

INTRODUCTION

I made a decision to write "What Does Self-Esteem Have To Do With Character" in the backdrop of encountering so many people who interact with condemnation, aggression, anger, hostility, guardedness, discouragement and depression. Similarly, the media has begun to bring to the forefront mental illness which has taken a sizable posture of how people are interacting as well, not to mention the problems of violence, social injustices, homelessness, and the inability for any number of people to secure suitable employment. In addition, there are many factors interfering with the wholeness of families, school safety and the safety of communities at large. Consequently, it is my belief there needs to be some form of remedies for such serious problems worldwide. Similarly, there are many hurting people in this world who are victims of domestic violence (to include incest, sexual abuse, verbal abuse, and physical abuse) as well as violence displayed throughout the world.

I wanted to address these cultural issues and their effects instead of just focusing on what they are, and it is my belief that people need a way out of situations as opposed to focusing on how bad things may appear to be. Thus, I chose to address these issues and provide some frameworks and formats of guidance in this book, "What Does Self-esteem Have To Do with Character?"

INFLUENCES EXERTED ON SELF-ESTEEM

The first experience with self-concept begins at birth and one's interaction with its family or caretaker(s) who sets the initial stage for the self-concept of a person that will be formed in the conscientious through interaction with family and or caretaker(s). If the interaction is one of negativity, condemnation, biasness, jealousy, dissatisfaction, negative comparisons, violence, or bullying; the tendency will become for that person to act out in ways that demonstrate those experiences, and inevitably cause destructive patterns of relating and low self-esteem.

As time goes on a person begins to interact and develop relationships with the family or caretaker(s) the self-concept deepens and the person will embrace their opinions, beliefs and gain an awareness of whom the family or caretaker(s) demonstrates they are. Therefore, a person's initial worth and value is formed through interaction with the family or caretaker(s). Similarly, our culture and spirituality also plays a role in developing self-concept. For instance culture can dictate how one should dress

1

to be acceptable, what is considered attractive by portraying such in the media.

In this present culture, there are movements which usher in detachment, being impersonal, lack of conscience, and the inability to create intimacy (non-sexual) as it relates to interacting with people. This present culture has given rise to the social media networks where any and all forms of information can be displayed and viewed by anyone, comments both negative and positive will be embraced. Thus, creating a culture that has become highly impersonal, insensitive, detached and without consciences.

In communities there is no bonding or fellowship. Therefore, most if not all of our problems derive from failure to have positive meaningful relationships, to be reconciled and restored in relationships. When these facts are analyzed it can readily be seen how these factors play out when there are problems in relationships, and how they eventually spill out affecting physical health and mental health. Many studies support facts that negative emotions are toxic and poisonous in our bodies causing numerous diseases.

Many times in life unpleasant and horrible things happen that are beyond our control. Things that are unjust, unfair, inconsiderate and beneath whom we really are. Things that are cruel, inhumane, unexplainable, and ones that cut and gnaw away our self-esteem. More often than not, these things happen to us through no fault of our own, through failure of being protected by significant persons in our lives, be it family or spouses, through a lack of provisions, through abuse of all types and natures, neglect, and not being valued as the human beings we actually are.

There are also negative cultural and social influences exerted upon people that impact one's mental stability as well, such as divorce, bullying, employment problems, socioeconomic inequality, death, illnesses and many other negative or overwhelming life experiences.

When horrible things happen to us in life not because we caused them, or incited them, there becomes a great deal of emotional trauma that gnaws away at our self-esteem and self-worth in having to deal with them. An even bigger problem arrives when there is a lack of support, a lack of access to meaningful help, and a lack of knowledge of how to effectively cope with day to day problems. Although, we did not cause these problems, or injustices, we are still held accountable for dealing with the issues.

We cannot learn in a stage of blaming, we must understand there is a period of appropriate blaming that does have to come to an end. We do have to take responsibility and deal with those happenings that are not our fault. We must assume responsibility for our attitudes and behaviors. It is a great insight to put into practice of while you may not be able to stop someone's behavior; you can definitely stop how you are affected by it.

We are not responsible for other's behaviors, nor can we control them, but we are directly responsible for our own attitudes and behaviors. Attempting to take responsibility for others often brings and adds much frustration and confusion within, thus lowering our own personal self-worth as an individual. It is extremely destructive to disown your own feelings, or put them on the back burner. We must recognize what we are feeling and deal with those feelings appropriately. To deny our feelings causes them to explode in other areas which is called displaced hostility.

Our attitudes, feelings, behaviors, thoughts, abilities, desires, and choices are all our personal identity and responsibility. When we fail to take responsibility for our behavior and put it in check, that is to control it; we will become powerless, dependent and hook up with people who will endorse, embrace and enable us to continue to demonstrate irresponsible behaviors. By doing so we will adopt a low self-image and remain broken. Subsequently, when one fails to take responsibility for their own behavior; it becomes necessary to make and take great escape routes and use mechanisms such as violence to resolve issues, drugs to deaden pain, and the adoption of compulsory behaviors; all of which eats directly at the soul, and gives a false sense of hopelessness and helplessness.

This present culture has opted out for extreme use of recreational and prescription drugs to deal with the distasteful happenings that come with life, as opposed to coping with the day to day problems which have caused massive decays in relationships. The failure to deal appropriately with these day-to-day problems; induces a high price where the effect will be paid and felt by children, relatives, friends, etc.

Taking responsibility for our feelings and not allowing someone else to control us with their feelings is what life is all about. There is a danger in trying to make everyone else happy because it promotes one to lose sight of self, and make decisions that are not in your best interest or well-being and forces one to become a people pleaser; all of which will eat away at having a healthy self-esteem.

REMEDY FOR A LOW SELF-ESTEEM

Self-esteem is life and death for anyone who is alive and will cause a person to speak, believe or act with behaviors that are negative or positive. A low self-esteem happens when one is not able to forgive one's self, holding on to resentment and bitterness about one's experiences, and toxic relationships whose purpose and design is to isolate support systems, tear down a person's worth, value and to destructively control that person.

An unhealthy self-concept also happens as a result of listening and allowing negative criticisms to take root in one's mind. Rehashing past disappointments, misunderstandings, failures, allowing human feelings and opinions to gain unhealthy recognition also adds to an unhealthy self-concept. It is imperative for one to develop a healthy self-esteem so that appropriate character will be adopted and respect for the rights of others will be displayed at all times.

When self-esteem is low a person becomes self-destructive, abusive, unapproachable and hostile; making it impossible to be included in any healthy relationship. A person with a low self-esteem will say bad things about themselves, will display that they do not like themselves, and will tend to believe they are not good enough to perform tasks.

A low self-esteem will cause others to distance and isolate themselves from that person with the low self-esteem for fear of having negative confrontations. When a person's self-esteem is low they cannot think appropriately but will believe everyone else is at fault and will blame others for their misfortunes never being able to face the fact their low self-esteem is causing problems but will consistently believe everyone is against them. When self-esteem is low the person is constantly angry without just causes and will respond defensively aggressive, and will be easily offended.

People with low self-esteem find it impossible to believe that God loves them but yet will attempt to love God with no expectation that He is loving and caring for them, and they are blessed of God as well. People with a low self-esteem are easily led into cults and destructive doctrines and are unable to really think for themselves. When a person's self-esteem is low they will accept anything because they believe this is the best they can have.

As you can see a low self-esteem is very dangerous to possess because it will immobilize you and keep you from ever coming into fruition and flourishing into the productive person you are capable of being.

It is erroneous to assume that we must only experience the pleasant aspects of life. Life in and of itself is made up of wonderful, distasteful and painful experiences. To deny this is to fail to face reality and risk mental illnesses. We must not attempt to categorize our lives by separating good and bad such that we have all bad things or only all good things that we experience as defining self as all good or all bad. Experiences good or bad cannot be allowed to define one's self. When experiences are allowed to define a person they become an emotional roller coaster, never fully recognizing who they are and what their potential actually is. Experiences are what happened in life only.

Experiences are not who a person is, only what happened to the person. This is a critical truth to embrace; without which, one will continually go back and forth looking for perfect relationships or situations and never being able to deal with obstacles, or happenings that create wonderful joys. The real problem is not being able to accept those experiences that life brings, but associating and allowing them to define one's being. Experiences must not be allowed to define a person's worth or value.

As human beings we were designed to be loved and to love, to care about and to be cared for. We were designed to have havens of safety and security. We were designed to have our basic needs met; which are physiological needs (food, shelter, clothing), safety needs, love and belonging needs, self-esteem needs, self-fulfillment needs, and knowledge needs. When a person is not getting their needs met, there will be both physical and mental health issues.

Mental health is being discussed in this book as the inability to cope appropriately with unfavorable circumstances and situations, the inability to display behavior that is socially acceptable, and the inability to control a behavior causing it to become compulsive addictive, which interferes with personal responsibilities, relationships, and health. Further, the intent is to expose the explosive effects on the inability to cope appropriately with life's changes. For the purpose of this book the mental health issues being discussed are those that causes mild to severe disturbances in thought and behavior, resulting in an inability to cope with ordinary demands and routines of life.

The inability to cope with life's ordinary demands is directly related to one's self-esteem.

Responding out of past injuries, our negative views of ourselves, our negative views of others and our negative views of God poses big time problems that must be addressed and places a demand that we must consider the consequences of how those responses will affect our mental and physical health, safety and families.

By refusing to accept good and bad from others; many individuals have destroyed many relationships which is really sad. By expecting people to be all good carries with that expectation a high risk of being utterly disappointed because the moment that person portrays something different we are going to reject them and burn the bridges. The inabilty to accept good and bad together is the greatest cause for broken relationships including divorce. That is not to say that we should tolerate any form of abuse. Actually, the tendency to see people as all bad is really a lack of love for that person.

Suffering is a necessary component in all our lives that will eventually promote growth, wisdom and knowledge. If we never suffer we will not have compassion or understanding for others, nor will we be able to identify, sympathize or en-courage others, we will have no background for pain.

It is one thing to behave with the intent to survive as a kid and totally and completely another to continue with these emotional survival skills as an adult; especially when they shut everyone else out. When one allows behaviors to continue in ways that makes it impossible and keeps us from entering into relationships with those we should love, then we are not coping in a legitimate way. Making attempts to avoid pain or to become protective of ourselves will not work, but rather has worked against oneself in the alternative, because it shuts out all of the true opportunities to be enjoyed, to enjoy, and the experience of real living and powerful relating.

We do not have the right as people and believers of God to shut down our functioning and become dead, refusing to love or reach out and touch people or to become a part of with the intent of improving situations. Therefore, when hurt and disappointment comes we do have the right to be sad, feel the pain of grief and sorrow and even groan inwardly, but even though these are necessary feelings to face what has happened there still needs to be the hope and the drive for something better. We must be mindful not to take the wrong route of "never again!" which causes contempt for others, and in addition to this stance, deaden the soul of going to a better choice of routes of choosing life, while at the same time recognizing the damage we have done to ourselves and others by being unapproachable and unlovable.

Nevertheless, to try to protect oneself from ever allowing yourselves to be treated like that again or hurt in that fashion again is futile as well because the very thing you are trying to protect yourself from which is actually being isolated and rejection is exactly what you fall into, so this tactic is no good as well. On the other hand, the reward of taking the biblical path to life is being free to love both God and our fellow man without dissimulation or fear, having a body that has a functioning soul that will reach out and touch or become a part of; which will make this a better world for all.

Putting on the victim mentality defensive armor will only add more pain to the soul and will strengthen the resolve of I will never be or let him or her hurt me again. Notwithstanding, the supposedly protection against pain does in fact intensifies the pain that it was supposed to shut down or make it go away. Therefore, whoever has caused pain cannot be allowed to be recognized as the enemy because that recognition will always give and keep an endless tie to that person. Consequently, the perpetrator must be dropped from the enemy's list, although he or she may be used by the enemy. The major enemy of our soul is unseen (Ephesians 6:10-13).

The quest is to get what is wrong inside fixed. For example let's take a peek of what actually happens to self-esteem when sexual abuse has occurred. Usually, the victim becomes the problem by the way they deal with the sexual abuse in and of itself. More often than not, because the victim isn't dealing with the act of sexual abuse which was not his or her fault appropriately, their lives will be characterized by continuous broken relationships, anger, hostility, loneliness, depression, outburst of aggressions eating disorders, promiscuity and the use of recreational drugs to deaden the pain. These expressions are understandable; however, they certainly are not acceptable behaviors. This is not to say this atrocious experience should be minimized. As horrible as it may be a sexual violation cannot be allowed to define a person in the negative.

There is healing for the victim, victory and ministry for the person as well. Thus, the remedy for a child of God's low self-esteem becomes the Word of God because God sent his Word and healed. In addition to, a renewing of the mind becomes necessary as well.

A renewed mind is done through reading God's Word

which will change how one thinks, acts, and will undo heavy burdens, remove guilt, destroy at the root bents of will and will replace negative habits with positive habits.

HOW DO I FORM A HEALTHY SELF IMAGE?

As a person matures one of the ways a healthy self-image can be formed is through having positive, healthy, and wholesome interactions with positive minded people, be it teachers, friends, ministers, or co-workers, etc. As a person matures they are not so inclined to allow the opinions of the family or caretaker(s) to dominate and dictate their worth and value.

The role spirituality plays in developing a healthy self-image is the most critical and essential element that it takes for each of us to grow emotional healthy. Failure to grow spiritually shows that one has closed all avenues to relationships and missed the entire mark of the reason for the gospel, which is to restore, and reconcile relationships, first to God then to our fellow man. When one fails to accept this key concept of the Gospel then emotional problems set in and one becomes self-destructive.

God has given us the greatest provision whereby each of us can have a healthy self-esteem. When we receive Him we become a new creature and all old thing are passed away (2

Corinthians 5:17) be it rape, crimes, abortions, or any type of violation. Not only so, God also declares that he has made us free (Romans 6:18) not set free but made us free which is quite a drastic difference. When someone has made something, then the recipient of that which was made had no choice in the matter of how the object was made, and it was done independently of their strength. The power of safe keeping, construction, deliverance and responsibility of that which was made rest in the hands of the one who made it.

Being set free is different and has its downfalls. Being set free becomes a choice of whether the person or thing wants to remain free or go back to the condition they were in before being set free. But when you are made free it is permanent and no one can undo it. "But now being made free from sin, and become servants to God, ye have your fruit unto holiness, and the end everlasting life. (Romans 6:22) Notwithstanding, in being made free God took another step to insure a healthy self-esteem by "Blotting out the handwriting of ordinances that was against us, which was contrary to us, and took it out of the way, nailing it to his cross;" (Colossian 2:14).

These are great truths to embrace and are guarantees for sound mental health. These truths should not be dismissed and not recognized for their healing virtue, but must be believed and applied to our everyday life.

For all practical purposes let's look at why this truth of being a new creature at the instance we receive Jesus Christ is so critical and must be believed, embraced, applied, and acted upon moment by moment in our lives. To accomplish this let's look at an example of a person who is guilty of murder and how this truth plays out. Paul the Apostle is a good example who declared in Galatians 1:13; and Acts 2:10-11, *"Ye have heard of my conversation in time past in the Jews religion, how beyond measure I persecuted the church of God and wasted it: Which thing I also did in Jerusalem: and many of the saints did I shut up in prison, having received authority from the chief priests; and when they were put to death, I gave my voice against them. And I punished them oft in every synagogue, and compelled them to blaspheme; and being exceedingly mad against them, I persecuted them even unto strange cities."*

With a natural eye and mind we believe and rightly so; a person who kills men and women for the sheer reason of not liking them because they are different or because they do not hold the same beliefs is a horrible insane, depraved, person and that they should be punished to the hilt. It is also reasonable to believe this person should be bound by a lot of guilt and could possibly injure themselves, and would have lots of sleepless nights. Equally so, it is reasonable to believe that a person like this is worthless and does not deserve to have any enjoyments of life. However, it becomes necessary to take a look at God's perspective of how He views a person who has committed such atrocities and one who has a horrible shameful past. To accomplish this, we hear God Himself declaring in Acts 9:15 "But the Lord said unto him, Go thy way: for he is a chosen vessel unto me, to bear my name before the Gentiles, and kings, and the children of Israel:" Translation, in spite of your past, God sees value and worth in you and will not hold your past against you, but frees you from it, lifts up your head (Psalms 3:3) places your feet on solid foundations, and establishes you among powers that be. (Ps. 40:2)

A second crucial look at a person who had an impressive pedigree and someone who had not given himself to low living, or spotted himself up such as Peter who declared he had never had any dealings with any form of uncleanness. However, Peter discovered when God declares he has made you clean no one has the ability to assert you as anything other than clean (What God hath cleansed, that call not thou common. Acts 10:15, 28) and Peter also later found out that God does not go by family pedigrees, a person's accomplishments or status in society (of a truth I perceive that God is no respecter of person: Acts 10:34.)

God is extremely sovereign and knows for a fact that horrible things happens to people unjustifiably so. Yet God declares that person is not the horrible thing that happened but possesses worth that God deems valuable. That's why it is necessary to walk in the newness of life that God has created for us thereby having made us new creatures and causing all old things to pass away and not allowing them to be attachable to us in God's frame work, nor credited to our account. We are to walk in newness of life and serve in the newness of spirit. Sometimes this truth is hard for many to embrace because they want to hold on to I have been raped, or I killed someone, how can it be that this is passed away? While it is true a rape occurred, or a child was born out of wedlock which cannot be denied, however, the trauma or sting of those acts cannot be sustained in the memory banks when God makes you a new creature. The trauma and sting is removed from the memory banks to such an extent you can walk in life without any further condemnation, fear or torment about those happenings. That's what God means when he declares "Old things are passed away", and you are a "new creature"! (2 Corinthians 5:17)

Guilt is a horrible punishment to carry around for the duration of a person's life, this why God created a way of escape for each of us to take so that we will not have to carry guilt by pining our guilt on the back of the Lord Jesus Christ. Isaiah 53:4 declares "Surely he (Jesus) hath borne our griefs, and carried our sorrows: yet we did esteem him stricken, smitten of God, and afflicted." Translation, we have been made free from the horrors, sorrow, and grief's of our past, as such, it is wasted energy to be brooding over what happened in our past because the Lord Jesus Christ, was wounded for our transgressions, *he was* bruised for our iniquities: the chastisement of our peace *was* upon him; and with his stripes we are healed Isaiah 53:5. This is why we can now declare without any form of fear that the we have sound minds, power over lies about who we once were and now also have the ability to be free to love (2 Timothy 1:7), and live our lives free from guilt over past misfortunes. (Romans 8:1-11)

WHAT TO DO WHEN PEOPLE ATTEMPT TO REMIND YOU OF YOUR PAST

It is our responsibility after being made a new creature in the Lord Christ Jesus to put into practice five basic but essential virtues, coupled with knowledge application of the Word of God and these are:

1. Put on the new man, which after God is created in righteousness and true holiness (Ephesians 4:24)

2. Put on the new man, which is renewed in knowledge after the image of him that created him: (Colossians 3:10)

3. Be not conformed to this world: but be ye transformed by the renewing of your mind, that ye may prove what is that good, and acceptable, and perfect, will of God. (Romans 12:2)

4. Recognize; There is therefore now no condemnation to them which are in Christ Jesus, who walk not after the flesh, but after the

Spirit. (Romans 8:1)

5. Recognize; Now we are delivered from the law, that being dead wherein we were held; that we should serve in newness of spirit, and not in the oldness of the letter. (Romans 7:6)

In putting on these five virtues we will be above the fray from people who will attempt to keep us in the past, and who do not have a clear understanding of the gospel of Jesus Christ, or understand what actually happens to a person when they receive Jesus Christ which is a regeneration that causes a new creation. Therefore, when a person does not have this understanding, ill attempts will be made to hold up prior life styles which really proves these type of people do not understand the purpose of grace and truth, or that when God makes us a new creation; our appetite for life styles of sinful practices changes, also our perspectives and priorities changes. I would even dare to say people who bring up your past haven't experienced the power of God. The power of God is so awesome and sovereign it takes a blinded person and gives sight, raises people from the dead, creates and rules in the affairs of men. I can safely say my life demonstrates the power and the ability of God. When people have not had such experiences with God; they will tend to throw up your past to you.

When People Reject You Because of Your Past

Many times in life we will be faced with rejections in various forms. One the most hurtful common types of rejection is one that entails your past. However, this type of rejection must not be allowed to take root in your memory banks Your identity cannot and must not rest in people's opinions, their rejections or their disagreements with you. Your identity must not and cannot be defined by unfavorable circumstances, the forces of darkness nor does your identity rest in family history.

When an attempt to reject you for your past is made you must recognize that you are not defined by your past but rather you are prepared by your past and your past has prepared you for your future. Not only so, the following principles must be applied immediately:

Recognition of the matchless redemptive work of the Lord Jesus Christ, that your identity rest in Him and that you must declare, embrace, and put on the following:

1. For in him we *live* and *move* and have our *being* Acts 17:28

   For ye are dead and your life is hid with Christ in God. Colossians 3:1

2. But as many as received him, to them gave he power to become the sons of God, even to them that believe on his name: John 1:12

3. Blessed be the God and Father of our Lord Jesus Christ, which according to his abundant mercy hath begotten us again unto a lively hope by the resurrection of Jesus Christ from the dead I Peter 1:3

4. In whom ye also trusted, after that ye heard the word of truth, the gospel of your salvation: in whom also after that ye believed, ye were sealed with that holy Spirit of promise Ephesians 1:13

Recognize And Believe You Are Full of Hope

To whom God would make known what is the riches of the glory of this mystery among the Gentiles; which is Christ in you, the hope of glory. Colossians 1:27

Note: Biblical hope means:

✓ Hope is no uncertainty whatsoever, sure and steadfast

✓ Hope is an anchor of the soul grounded, established, settled and rooted in God's word upon which I can lay hold on and which in turn will lay hold on me.

✓ Hope is when I am faced with difficulties I know the hope God has given me does entereth into that (God's presence) within the veil; giving me boldness to do so!

✓ Hope is what I know to be true. (Hebrews 6:19-20)

Recognize And Believe You Are Righteous And Justified

For he hath made him to be sin for us, who knew no sin; that we might be made the righteousness of God in him. 2 Corinthians 5:21

Even the righteousness of God which is by faith of Jesus Christ unto all and upon all them that believe: Romans 3:22. Therefore being justified by faith, we have peace with God through our Lord Jesus Christ. Romans 5:1

Recognize And Believe You Reign in Life

For if by one man's offence death reigned by one; much more they which receive abundance of grace and of the gift of righteousness shall reign in life by one, Jesus Christ. Romans 5:17

My grace is sufficient for thee; for my strength is made perfect in weakness 2 Corinthians 12:9

And now I commend you to God and to the word of

his grace, which is able to build you up and to give you the inheritance among all those who are sanctified Acts 20:32

Recognize And Believe You Are Established

In righteousness shalt thou be established: thou shall be far from oppression; for thou shall not fear; and from terror; for it shall not come near thee. Isaiah 54:14

He brought me up also out of an horrible pit, out of the miry clay, and set my feet upon a rock, and established my goings. Psalms 40:2

Now therefore ye are no more strangers and foreigners, but fellow citizens with the saints, and of the household of God; Ephesians 2:19

Recognize And Believe You Are Prosperous, Healthy, And You Got Favor

...I wish above all things that thou mayest prosper and be in health, even as thy soul prospereth 3 John 1:2

The blessing of the Lord, it maketh rich, and he addeth no sorrow with it. Proverbs 10: 22

For thou Lord *wilt* bless the righteous: with favor will thou compass him as with a shield Psalms 5:12

Recognize And Believe You Are Blessed, Seated With Jesus, No More A Stranger

Blessed be the God and Father of our Lord Jesus Christ, who hath blessed us with all spiritual blessings in heavenly places in Christ Ephesians 1:3

And hath raised us up together, and made us sit together in heavenly places in Christ Jesus: Ephesians 2:6

Now therefore ye are no more strangers and foreigners but fellowcitizens with the saints and of the household of God Ephesians 2:19

Recognize And Believe You Are Redeemed

In whom we have redemption through his blood the for-giveness of sins according to the riches of his grace. Ephesians 1:7

In whom we have redemption through his blood, even the forgiveness of sins: Colossians 1:14

Recognize And Believe You Are A Joint Heir, Plus You Have An Inheritance Too

And if children, then heirs; heirs of God, and joint-heirs with Christ; if so be that we suffer with him, so that we may be also glorified together Romans 8:17

To an inheritance incorruptible, and undefiled, and that fadeth not away, reserved in heaven for you, 1 Peter 1:4

The eyes of your understanding being enlightened; that ye may know what is the hope of his calling, and what the riches of the glory of his inheritance in the saints, Ephesians 1:18

Giving thanks unto the Father, which hath made us meet to be partakers of the inheritance of the saints in light Colossians.1:12

Knowing that of the Lord ye shall receive the reward of the inheritance: for ye serve the Lord Christ. Colossians 3:24

In whom also we have obtained an inheritance, being predestinated according to the purpose of him who worketh all things after the counsel of his own will Ephesians 1:11

And for this cause he is the mediator of the New Testament, that by means of death, for the redemption of the transgressions that were under the first testament, they which are called might receive the promise of eternal inheritance. Hebrews 9:15

Recognize And Believe You Are Strengthened

Strengthened with all might, according to his glorious power, unto all patience and longsuffering with joyfulness Colossians 1:11

I can do all things through Christ which strengtheneth me. Philippians 4:13

Recognize And Believe You Are An Overcomer, Victorious, A Conqueror, And Triumphant

For whatsoever is born of God *overcometh* the world:

and this is the victory that overcometh the world, even our faith. 1 John 5:4

But thanks be to God, which giveth us the *victory* through our Lord Jesus Christ. 1 Corinthians 15:57

Nay, in all these things we are more than *conquerors* through him that love us Romans 8:37

Thanks be unto God who always causes me to triumph 2 Corinthians 2:14

Recognize And Believe You Are Bold, Confident, And Have Confidence

Having therefore, brethren boldness to enter into the holiest by the blood of Jesus Hebrews 10:19

In whom we have boldness and access with confidence by the faith of him. Ephesians 3:12

Being confident of this very thing, that he which hath begun a good work in you will perform it until the day of Jesus Christ: Philippians 1:6

For God hath not given us the spirit of fear; but of power, and of love, and of a sound mind. 2 Timothy 1:7

For we have not an high priest which cannot be touched with the feeling of our infirmities; but was in all points tempted like as we are, yet without sin. Hebrews 4:15

Let us therefore come boldly unto the throne of grace,

that we may obtain mercy, and find grace to help in time of need. Hebrews 4:16

Recognize And Believe You Are A Mighty Warrior Who Stands Against, Withstands, Stands, And Stand Therefore!

For the weapons of our warfare *are* not carnal, but mighty through God to the pulling down of strong holds; 2 Cor. 10:4

Put on the whole armour of God, that ye may be able to stand (1) against the wiles of the devil (2) principalities (3) powers (4) rulers of the darkness of this world (5) spiritual wickedness in high places Ephesians 6:11 (5 stand against) Wherefore take unto you the whole armour of God, that ye may be able to withstand in the evil day, and having done all, to stand Ephesians 6:13

Stand therefore, having your loins girt about with truth, and having on the breastplate of righteousness; Ephesians 6:14

Recognize And Believe You Are Whole, Accepted And Perfected

And ye are complete in him, which is the head of all principality and power Colossians 2:10

To the praise of the glory of his grace, wherein he hath made us accepted in the beloved Ephesians 1:6

For by one offering he hath perfected for ever them that are sanctified... Hebrews 10:14

Whereof the Holy Ghost also is a witness to us Hebrews 10:14-15 (Translation when you are baptized with the Holy Ghost that is your witness you are perfect)

Recognize And Believe You Are Secure

There is therefore now no condemnation to them which are in Christ Jesus, who walk not after the flesh, but after the Spirit. Romans 8:1

Recognize And Believe You Have Nothing To Be Ashamed About

For I am not ashamed of the gospel of Christ: for it is the power of God unto salvation to every one that believeth; to the Jew first, and also to the Greek. Romans 1:16

Be not thou therefore ashamed of the testimony of our Lord, nor of me his prisoner: but be thou partaker of the afflictions of the gospel according to the power of God; 2 Timothy 1:8

Who hath saved us, and called us with an holy calling, not according to our works, but according to his own purpose and grace, which was given us in Christ Jesus before the world began, 2 Timothy 1:9

For the which cause I also suffer these things:

nevertheless I am not ashamed: for I know whom I have believed, and am persuaded that he is able to keep that which I have committed unto him against that day. 2 Timothy 1:12

NECESSITY FOR HEALTHY RELATIONSHIPS ON SELF-IMAGE

We were not created to be an island. God meant for us to be relational to Him and to others. The whole creation is named after God (Ephesians 3:15). God created us with a hunger to fellowship with Him and others and fellowship is a basic need. Jesus is the true vine and we are the branches, nothing in and of itself exist without nutrition and nurturing. We are forgiven when we forgive others.

The necessity for healthy relationships is called bonding. Bonding is essential from the exiting of the womb to the entrance of the grave. Without bonding people become sick, mentally ill and dysfunctional. Our inability to bond often affects our health. The benefits of bonding helps us to become and remain moral and loyal, it helps us through stressful times and allows us to be transparent enough to reveal problems and get support. Finally, bonding is a blessing because it allows us to share our earthly goods and accomplishment with someone, which gives them meaning.

When effective bonding is not apparent; depression and despair sets in. Although bonding is a basic need and the answer to all our ills be it spiritual or emotionally, there are a number of things that keeps us from bonding such as pain not being able to get over someone's betrayal, or disappointment. As long as we act like or believe that what someone has done unfavorably to us is the problem; it will hold us back from getting on with our lives, and we will never be able to take the key and unlock the doors to real life. Therefore, one must overcome all unfavorable happenings or die from them.

If we judge all of our future experience on the one bad past one; we shut the door, lock it and throw away the key. Memories work for and against us and it is a given that disappointments in all shapes and forms will or has come. We have to move forward and try again. While we are correct in not opening up to known blatant abusers, deceiver or be-trayers that is not to say that we then have the right to shut everyone else out thereafter based on the past unfavorable experiences.

In order for any type of healing or change to occur, we must open up to a relationship and trust yet verifying. It is true that some relationships are not good, nor safe, but when we fail to bond completely it is not only hazardous to ourselves but it is also devastating to others. We have to see ourselves as God see us; he values us, trust us, want us and need us. We have to recognize that we are of value and loved. We do not have the right to get our godly given needs met in ungodly ways. We do need to be selective in choosing our relationships such that we chose ones that will build us up into the image of God, rather than tearing us down.

Developing bonding skills rest on the recognition that each of us have a real live need to be a part of or bond with someone, and we should make a move toward this end. As Proverbs 18:24 declares "A man that hath friends," must first show yourself friendly to attract and maintain friends. In order for bonding to take place becoming transparent and open for attack is essential or we will die never knowing what it was like to have loved and lost. You cannot afford to play it safe when it comes to bonding. We must get rid of distorted thinking about betrayal, and take a risk with people. Learning to bond takes time, knowledge, wisdom, and understanding of God's graces and his truths.

The Inability to Set Boundaries

There is a tremendous need to set boundaries in bonding, and that one must set limits on other's control of their time, talents and abilities. We must recognize our personal space and boundaries. When we are unable to set boundaries it sets us up to be abused and used for someone else's gain. One must discover that becoming an adult is an awesome task because we must gain competencies in specific areas of our lives, gain control of our lives, and accomplish this without causing conflict. In order to develop into emotionally healthy and productive people, we must begin with bonding, setting boundaries, being able to have our individuality, resolve hurts, unfavorable relationship, and injustices.

Our identities are formed as a result of our beliefs, talents, abilities, attitudes, and feelings. We are not who people say we are, we are who God says we are. It is imperative that we set boundaries for our own personal well being. God expects us to take personal responsibility for our beliefs and attitudes and not let others define us. God gives us freedom to be ourselves. His word declares that each of us are different, have different gifts and task to perform. We should use care to be sure that we are being transformed into the image of God as opposed to adopting the opinion of others. (1Corinthians 12:7-11; 28-30)

If we are going to be able to set boundaries then we must own up to our behavior. The two principles that clear up any identify crisis are (1) I am not responsible for other's behavior and (2) I cannot blame others for my behaviors. Another facet of setting a boundary lends itself to our thought processes that exist within us. Our thoughts are hidden from everyone except God and they are a part of who we are. We are to guard our heart for out of it are the issues of life (Proverbs 4:23). It is equally important not to put ourselves in positions where we are brain washed into thinking other's thoughts to be accepted by them. Thinking for yourself is necessary to your identity and freedom and a strong boundary must be set to protect our thinking. Likewise, our abilities and talents lie in the domain of our thought process. It is important to abide in your own calling as oppose to conforming to other's dreams and desire for you. When you choose an out of field talent based on someone else's dream for you, it lends itself to nothing but failure and frustration.

Desires are another important facet of our set-ting boundaries. However, even after recognition of our desires, we are to acknowledge the Lord in all our ways and he will direct our path (Proverbs 3:5-6). Being able to make our own choices is vital to setting boundaries. If we do not take responsibility for our choices, we will have a tendency to blame and hold resentment for the person we believe made choices for us. Our choices determine our directions. We also have to be watchful of setting limits as well, and not over extending ourselves, God is infinite only, and we are finite.

Finally, an important aspect of our identity and ability to set boundaries is being able to say no. Saying no is an essential element of being me (who I am), not being able to take responsibility for saying you can count me out ends up with you not being yourself, but a puppet on a string. There is a difference in being responsible to one than from being responsible for one and we must know when and how to identify that difference and how to respond and learn that it is okay to say no even to your children and that you do not have to feel guilty for saying no to anyone. Actually, being able to say no is a form of protection for oneself. Many people have taken dangerous paths that led to losses, self-destruction, and financial ruin because they were unable to say to no to someone.

WHAT IS CHARACTER?

The word character comes from the Greek *kharakter* for "engraved mark," "symbol or imprint on the soul," and "instrument for marking." A colloquial definition for character is what you do when no one is looking. A standing cliché of describing character is "if you don't stand for something you will fall for anything," and Webster's New College Dictionary defines character as "moral strength, self-discipline, and a statement about behavior." With these working definitions it is safe to declare that your dealings with others will display what type of character you have, be it disingenuous or impeccable. As such, character is not a person's personal tastes (dress, preferences in food, car, homes, etc.) or, personality (temperament, outgoing, quiet, etc.). Character has more to do with a person's thought processes, choices, integrity, motives, bents of will, morals and habits which produces various outcomes such as, shady dealings, shades of grey, integrity or outstanding behaviors in difficult circumstances. Therefore, one's self-esteem has everything to do with character because if you do not believe you have an individual worth and value you will be prone to adopt the views others have of you and will act accordingly.

Who Are You?

How would you answer if and when you are asked who are you? Your answer to this question will be reflective of your self-esteem and character. It will also demonstrate what you believe about yourself and the Word of God.

When you answered the question of who are you? Did you answer from a sin consciousness or did you answer it from a righteousness consciousness or did you behave like an orphan (not recognizing God as your Father and the intimacy we have with him)?

Let's look at the difference between a sin consciousness and righteousness consciousness. Romans 5:17 declares when we receive (continually second by second) of the gift of righteousness, we shall reign in life. Meaning we will not be prone to allow the enemy to use a performance record against us and beat us over the head with guilt about our past failure (condemnation), but will constantly stand on the Word of God that we are righteous through and because of the Blood of Jesus Christ (Ephesians 2:13-14) plus nothing else; just the Blood of Jesus Christ alone. We cannot afford to have a lack of truth within us concerning God's Word about our righteousness, or a lack of applying the truth of God's Word about our righteousness because the enemy will attempt to sow seeds with the intent of making us feel, believe, and act like what Jesus did on the cross was not enough and that we must have some type of performance record to prove who we are.

We all know that the devil is a liar and the father of lies (John 8:44); "Ye are of *your* father the devil, and the lusts of your father ye will do. He was a murderer from the beginning, and abode not in the truth, because there is no truth in him. When he speaketh a lie, he speaketh of his own: for he is a liar, and the father of it." As result of the devil being a liar; he has down played the fact of our righteousness in Christ Jesus to the extent there is so much disputing about being righteous and perfect even to the point many believers will state it is not true that we are righteous and perfect. But we must come to a position of whose report we are going to believe. It has to be one or the other; we are righteous solely because of the Blood or Jesus, or the Blood of Jesus is not enough to declare a person righteous and perfect. This lack of truth does directly affect one's self-esteem and thereby diminishes one's character as well.

Hindrances to Healthy Self-Esteem

We may as well face some facts here about our thinking. Our thinking is critical to our well being because it determines how we will act. It is impossible to obtain and display appropriate character when we think wrong. For instance; if you are unable to believe (thinking and acting) that you have access to God with confidence (Ephesians 3:12; Hebrew 4:16) you will constantly ask those whom you believe have some type of special access to God to pray for you, being unable to accept the fact that you can go to God for yourself at any time and he will hear you, and not hear someone else better for you. As a result you will never be able to enter into the joys of personal intimacy with God. (Proverbs 23:7 For as he thinketh in his heart, so *is* he:) So what kind of character and self-esteem is a person displaying when they cannot believe they are qualified to have access to God with confidence?

Another major problem to having a healthy self-esteem and character is for us to compare ourselves one to the other. Comparing oneself to another is a big mistake because you only see the glory the person now stands in but you do not know the story behind that glory. When people understand the losses, the pain, the loneliness, the misunderstanding a person's has gone through to get the glory then you will suddenly change your mind about wanting to be like that person. There is an old song that says "I want to be just like Him (Jesus) when he comes," but when homelessness hits, betrayal comes, rejection surfaces, etc., we quickly change our mind about wanting to be just like Jesus. You must be very careful not to compare yourself because comparing yourself to another minimizes your individuality, creativity and tends to make you feel less than, not good enough, helpless and worthless. These are not feelings that are inspired from God. "For we dare not make ourselves of the number, or compare ourselves with some that commend themselves: but they measuring themselves by themselves, and comparing themselves among themselves are not wise" (Corinthians 10:12).

Dissatisfaction with ourselves; what we look like, what we have or don't have, etc., is another big problem that causes strife, and restlessness which spills out into our relationships with others and makes one hard to get along with. Dissatisfaction with oneself is a useless and destructive emotion which has caused many to become injurious to themselves and others. "From whence *come* wars and fightings among you? *come they* not hence, *even* of your lusts that war in your members?" (James 4: 1) "Ye lust, and have not: ye kill, and desire to have, and cannot obtain: ye fight and war, yet ye have not, because ye ask not." James 4: 2

Jealousy is a drastic and dangerous hindrance to a healthy self-esteem and character. Jealousy has caused many to commit crimes of passions, caused many to destroy someone's influence and reputation. Jealousy has caused losses of all shapes and forms, and jealousy has caused great divides in families and communities. The issue behind jealousy is a person's low self-esteem. "Jealousy *is* cruel as the grave: the coals thereof *are* coals of fire, *which hath a* most vehement flame." Solomon 8:6

I like the definition that Wikipedia gives for jealousy. "Jealousy is an emotion, and the word typically refers to the negative thoughts and feelings of insecurity, fear, and anxiety over an anticipated loss of something of great personal value, particularly in reference to a human connection. Jealousy often consists of a combination of emotions such as anger, resentment, inadequacy, helplessness and disgust." For practical purposes I will translate jealousy into a simple expression of jealousy wants to keep and envy wants to have. This is why jealousy is so dangerous because it will go to any length to keep and the end result of jealousy is losses of enjoyments of life and in many cases loss of life.

To get control of our lives we must own up to our own behavior. Covering for other's behavior only temporarily suspend the consequences and make us more dependent, thereby creating more problems of dependency on the enabler. A healthy self-esteem and healthy character controls our thoughts which in turn dictates our growth. Therefore, we must take responsibility for our thought process. If not, thoughts will affect our interpersonal relating.

Trying to adjust ourselves because of what people think is a mistake and promotes a low self-esteem; people have the freedom to think what they will or may. There is no room in the believer's life for fearing what others think of you. We must accept their ability to be critical. However, to be self-condemning in our thoughts of ourselves has no place. We all have the God given right to make our own choices right or wrong. God give us space to set limits on ourselves as well as setting limits on how we will be affected by other's behavior or what they think of us.

A healthy self-esteem goes to viewing our failures in a realistic loving manner which induces reality, but when we view them with condemnation we tend to hide things. Hiding things impedes the healthy development of character. So in essence it does not do any good to hide things. We were not made to hide and harbor sin, but rather to accept the redemptive work of the Lord Jesus Christ to deliver us from sin. Jesus became a curse for us, such that we would not have to walk in a cursed life. Forgiveness of one's self and others frees us from both the perpetrator and our own self. Unforgiveness forever ties us to both the perpetrator and the horrors of our past failures, losses and weakness, etc. Consequently, confessing, forgiving and prayer will also help us develop a healthy self-esteem.

A part of having a healthy self-esteem and sound character comes into play when we relate to people we are to see ourselves as equal to them and not below them. As adults we must take charge of our lives and not allow others to make us believe we are beneath them and thus become people pleasers. We must seek to please God, which makes all the difference in the world of who is actually in charge of our lives, or who we are under. We must not embrace fallacious views of God's Word, nor become willing to listen to erroneous information.

Needing the approval of others conflicts many times with the will of God for our lives. God has given us authority and expects us to use it responsibly and freely, yet we must be yielded and submitted to God. This is good news to recognize that because of the fall we lost the ability to have freedom to take charge of our lives, but because of the redemptive work and supreme sacrifice of our Lord Jesus Christ and the shedding of his blood we now have power with freedom to take charge of our lives. We are no more slaves to sin but now have been given the spirit of power, spirit of love and the spirit of a sound mind (2 Timothy 1:7) to stand and withstand the wiles of the enemy.

HOW TO OVERCOME INSECURITY, AND NOT LET ANYONE DEFINE YOU

Examine yourselves, whether ye be in the faith; prove your own selves. Know ye not your own selves, how that Jesus Christ is in you, except ye be reprobates?
2 Corinthians 13:5

To whom God would make known what is the riches of the glory of this mystery among the Gentiles; which is Christ in you, the hope of glory: Colossians 1:27

For in him we live, and move, and have our being; as certain also of your own poets have said, For we are also his offspring Acts 17:28

Therefore if any man be in Christ, he is a new creature: old things are passed away; behold, all things are become new. 2 Corinthians 5:17

And that ye put on the new man, which after God is created in righteousness and true holiness. Ephesians 4:24

For by one offering he hath perfected for ever them that are sanctified Hebrews 10:14

Whereof the Holy Ghost also is a witness to us: for after that he had said before, Hebrews 10:15

And ye are complete in him, which is the head of all principality and power Colossians 2:10

Being confident of this very thing, that he which hath begun a good work in you will perform it until the day of Jesus Christ. Philippians 1:6

And hath raised us up together, and *made* us sit together in heavenly places in Christ Jesus Ephesians 2:6

There is therefore now no condemnation for those which are in Christ Jesus, who walk not after the flesh, but after the Spirit. Romans 8:1

But ye are not in the flesh, but in the Spirit, if so be that the Spirit of God dwell in you. Now if any man have not the Spirit of Christ, he is none of his. Romans 8:9

In whom we have *boldness* and access with confidence by the faith of him Ephesians 3:12

For we have not an high priest which cannot be touched with the feeling of our infirmities; but was in all points tempted like as we are, yet without sin. Let us therefore come *boldly* unto the throne of grace, that we may obtain mercy, and find grace to help in time of need. Hebrews 4:15-16

God says "I will never leave thee nor forsake thee!" Hebrews 13:5

Strengthened with all might, according to his glorious power, unto all patience and longsuffering with joyfulness Colossians 1:11

For you are dead, and your life is hid with Christ in God. Colossians 3:3

For the law of the Spirit of Life in Christ Jesus hath made me free from the law of sin and death! Romans 8: 2

Christ hath redeemed us from the curse of the law, being made a curse for us: for it is written, Cursed is every one that hangeth on a tree: Galatians 3:13

That we should be to the praise of his glory, who first trusted in Christ. In whom ye also trusted, *after* that ye heard the word of truth, the gospel of your salvation: in whom also after that ye believed, ye were sealed with the holy Spirit of promise. Ephesians 1:12

Which is the earnest of our inheritance until the redemption of the purchase possession, unto the praise of his glory! Ephesians 1:14

Now unto him that is able to keep you from falling, and to

present *you* faultless before the presence of his glory with exceeding joy. Jude 1:24-25

Let the redeemed of the Lord say so, whom he hath redeemed from the hand of the enemy Psalms 107:2

Cast not away therefore your confidence, which hath great recompense of reward. Hebrews 10:35

For God hath not given us the spirit of fear; but of power, and of love and of a sound mind. 2 Timothy 1:7

For ye have not received the spirit of bondage again to fear; but ye have received the spirit of adoption whereby we cry, Abba, Father. Romans 8:15

Peace I leave with you; my peace I give unto you: not as the world giveth, give I unto you. Let not your heart be troubled, neither let it be afraid John 14:27

Thou wilt keep him in perfect peace, whose mind is stayed on thee: because he trusteth in thee. Isaiah 26:3

For whatsoever is born of God overcometh the world: and this is the victory that overcometh the world, even our faith. 1 John 5:4

I can do all things through Christ who strengthens me Philippians 4:13

For with God nothing shall be impossible with God. Luke 1:37

If you abide in me and my words abide in you, ye shall ask what ye will, and it shall be done unto you John 15:7

But thou, O Lord, art a shield for me; my glory, and the lifter up of my head Psalm 3:3

Trust ye in the Lord for ever: for in the Lord Jehovah is everlasting strength: Isaiah 26:4

Wherefore I perceive that there is nothing better, than that a man should rejoice in his own works: for that is his portion: for who shall bring him to see what shall be after him? Ecclesiastes 3:22

Every man also to whom God hath given riches and wealth, and hath given him power to eat thereof, and to take his portion, and to rejoice in his labour; this is the gift of God. Ecclesiastes 5:19

GOD'S INFALLIBLE PROOFS, SECURITIES AND ASSURANCES

MAJOR SECURITY FOR ETERNAL LIFE

And I give unto them eternal life; and they shall never perish, neither shall any man pluck them out of my hand. John 10:28

Wherefore he is able also to save them to the uttermost that come unto God by him, seeing he ever liveth to make intercession for them. Hebrews 7:25

In whom ye also trusted, after that ye heard the word of truth, the gospel of your salvation: in whom also after that ye believed, ye were sealed with that Holy Spirit of promise Ephesians 1:13

Let us draw near with a true heart in full assurance of faith, having our hearts sprinkled from an evil conscience, and our bodies washed with pure water. Hebrews 10:22

Therefore: Let us hold fast the profession of our faith without wavering; for he is faithful that promised; Hebrews 10:23

Cast not away therefore your confidence, which hath great recompence of reward. Hebrews 10:35

MAJOR SECURITY FOR THE BAPTISM OF THE HOLY GHOST

For by one offering he hath perfected for ever them that are sanctified. Hebrews 10:14

Whereof the Holy Ghost also *is a* witness to us: for after that he had said before, Hebrews 10:15

This is the covenant that I will make with them after those days, saith the Lord, I will put my laws into their hearts, and in their minds will I write them; Hebrews 10:16

And their sins and iniquities will I remember no more. Hebrews 10:17

MAJOR SECURITY AND ASSURANCE FOR WHO YOU ARE IN GOD

Therefore if any man be in Christ, he is a new creature: old things are passed away; behold, all things are become new. 2 Corinthians 5:17 (mental health, self-esteem)

Therefore we are buried with him by baptism into death: that like as Christ was raised up from the dead by the glory of the Father, even so we also should walk in newness of life. Romans 6:4

But now we are delivered from the law, that being dead wherein we were held; that we should serve in newness of spirit, and not in the oldness of the letter. Romans 7:6

For in Christ Jesus neither circumcision availeth any thing, nor uncircumcision, but a new creature. Galatians 6:15

And that ye put on the new man, which after God is created in righteousness and true holiness. Ephesians 4:24 (mental health, self-esteem)

And have put on the new man, which is renewed in knowledge after the image of him that created him: Colossians 3:10

MAJOR SECURITIES AND ASSURANCES FOR ACCESS TO GOD

In whom we have boldness and access with confidence by the faith of him. Ephesians 3:12

Having therefore, brethren, boldness to enter into the holiest by the blood of Jesus, Hebrews 10:19

By a new and living way, which he hath consecrated for us, through the veil, that is to say, his flesh; Hebrews 10:20

And the veil of the temple was rent in twain from the top to the bottom. Matthews 15:38

MAJOR SECURITIES AND ASSURANCES OF JESUS AND THE HOLY GHOST PRAYING FOR YOU

NOTE: Jesus ever liveth to make intercession for you daily!

Wherefore he is able also to save them to the uttermost that come unto God by him, seeing he ever liveth to make intercession for them. Hebrews 7:25

And now I am no more in the world, but these are in the world, and I come to thee. Holy Father, keep through thine own name those whom thou hast given me, that they may be one, as we are. John 17:11

I pray not that thou shouldest take them out of the world, but that thou shouldest keep them from the evil. John 17:15

Father, I will that they also, whom thou hast given me, be with me where I am; that they may behold my glory, which thou hast given me: for thou lovedst me before the foundation of the world. John 17:24

Likewise the Spirit also helpeth our infirmities: for we know not what we should pray for as we ought: but the Spirit itself maketh intercession for us with groanings which cannot be uttered. Romans 8:26

MAJOR SECURITIES AND ASSURANCES MY PRAYERS ARE PRECIOUS TO GOD

And when he had taken the book, the four beasts and four and twenty elders fell down before the Lamb, having every one of them harps, and golden vials full of odours, which are the prayers of saints. Revelation 5:8

And another angel came and stood at the altar, having a golden censer; and there was given unto him much incense, that he should offer it with the prayers of all saints upon the golden altar which was before the throne. Revelation. 8:3

And the smoke of the incense, which came with the prayers of the saints, ascended up before God out of the angel's hand Revelation 8:4

MAJOR SECURITY OF SIN BEING TAKEN CARE OF PAST, PRESENT AND FUTURE FOR THE BELIEVER

For by one offering he hath perfected for ever them that are sanctified. Hebrews 10:14

How much more shall the blood of Christ, who through the eternal Spirit offered himself without spot to God, purge your conscience from dead works to serve the living God? (mental health, self-esteem) Hebrews 9:14

For Christ is not entered into the holy places made with hands, which are the figures of the true; but into heaven itself, now to appear in the presence of God for us: Hebrews 9:24

Nor yet that he should offer himself often, as the high priest entereth into the holy place every year with blood of others; Hebrews 9:25

For then must he often have suffered since the foundation of the world: but now once in the end of the world hath he appeared to put away sin by the sacrifice of himself. Hebrews 9:26

And as it is appointed unto men once to die, but after this the judgment: Hebrews 9:27

So Christ was once offered to bear the sins of many; and unto them that look for him shall he appear the second time without sin unto salvation. Hebrews 9:28

MAJOR POINTS OF JESUS' PRIESTLY MINISTRY AT THE RIGHT HAND OF GOD NOW!
(High Priest, Minister, Mediator, Advocate)

Now of the things which we have spoken this is the sum: We have such an high priest, who is set on the right hand of the throne of the Majesty in the heavens; Romans 8:1

A minister of the sanctuary, and of the true tabernacle, which the Lord pitched, and not man. Romans 8:2

But now hath he obtained a more excellent ministry, by how much also he is the mediator of a better covenant, which was established upon better promises. Romans 8:6

But this man, after he had offered one sacrifice for sins forever, sat down on the right hand of God; Hebrews 10:12

ATTITUDE ABOUT MY TRIALS

Points: My faith is crucial during trials because I must use it to resist the enemy steadfastly. My faith is a life or death issue; without faith it is impossible to please God!

NT Terms Used for Christian/Saints Walk with God

Soldier, fight the good fight of faith, put on the whole armor of God, fight, strive, conquer, overcome, victory. These are war terms used in the Bible to describe our walk with God. Not only so, we possess weapons for warfare associated with a solider which are: helmet, shields, swords, girted with truth, weapons mighty through God (Ephesians 6:10, 2 Corinthians 10:4)

POSITIONS AND STANCES I AM TO TAKE FIRST AND FOREMOST

Fight For My Faith - What I Believe Is Critical!

✓Fight the good fight of faith 1 Timothy 6:12 v
✓Whom resist steadfast in the faith 1 Peter 5:9-10

Being established in the faith that I am *made right* with God through Jesus' blood. Acts 16:5; Hebrews 10:19; Ephesians 2:13;

- ✓That I am the righteousness of God in Christ. (2 Corinthians 5:21) and

- ✓...they which receive abundance of grace and of the gift of righteousness shall reign in life by one Jesus Christ! Romans 5:17

NOTE:

My heart cannot be persuaded to be discouraged, intimidated, or manipulated, if it is steadfast in the faith, and is established in the righteousness God has provided for me because God says:

- ▸ In righteousness *shall* thou be established: "You shall be far from oppression; for you shall not fear: and from terror; for it shall not come near you". (Isaiah 54:14)

- ▸ God will keep me in perfect peace; when my mind is stayed on him Isaiah 26:3

- ▸ Rooted, and built up in him, and stablished in the faith, as ye have been taught, abounding therein with thanksgiving. Colossians 2:7

POINTS:

1. Because my heart is now established in righteousness, I can boldly declare, and agree with God that although I may have problems in my life, I am not guilty in God's eyes. I am justified in God's eyes by faith because of Jesus' redemptive work. I am righteous by Jesus' blood!

2. Problems do not mean I am doing something wrong or sinning

3. *I am not condemned!* - regardless of how things may look or what things may feel like (Romans 8:1) because I am justified by faith which has given me peace with God through our Lord Jesus Christ Romans 5:1

4. I have been baptized with the Holy Ghost who declares (is a witness) that I am perfect Hebrews 10:14-15; In light of this declaration how can I be condemned?

5. Now I am perfect through the blood of Jesus Christ when God looks at me that's all he can see is Jesus' blood; he cannot and will not look beyond or through the blood of Jesus only at it!

MY ATTITUDE (all mental - is my faith)

▸ Know I am kept by the power of God through *faith* 1 Peter 1:5

▸ Know that the trial of my faith is:

    a) More precious than gold that perish

    b) My faith might be found unto praise and honor and glory at the appearing of Jesus Christ 1 Peter 1:7

▸ Endure grief suffering wrongfully 1 Peter 2:19

▸ Know it is acceptable to God for me take suffering wrongfully patiently

Know Jesus is my example:

1. I must follow in his footsteps 1 Peter 2: 21

2. Because Jesus did not sin no guile was found in his mouth 1 Peter 2: 22

3. When he suffered he did not *threaten* people 1 Peter 2:23

NOTE:

Who his own self bare our sins in his own body on the tree, that we, being dead to sins, should live unto righteousness:

by whose stripes ye were healed.

▸ Know if I suffer for righteousness' sake; I should be happy not upset or trying to get even 1 Peter 3:15

▸ Know it is Better if the will of the God be so, that you suffer for well doing, than for evil doing 1 Peter 3:17

▸ Know that he that suffered in the flesh hath ceased from sin 1 Peter 4:1. Because Jesus suffered for us I must:

   a) Arm myself with the same mind that I must suffer also

   b) Because I have ceased from sin; I don't live in the flesh but to the will of God 1 Peter 4:2

▸ Know that I must go through much tribulation Acts 14:22 Confirming the souls of the disciples, and exhorting them to continue in the faith, and that we must through much tribulation enter into the kingdom of God

▸ Know that I am to be rejoicing in hope; patient in tribulation; continuing instant in prayer; Romans 12:12

▸ Know and remember that God Who comforteth us in all our tribulation, that we may be able to comfort them which are in any trouble, by the comfort wherewith we ourselves are comforted of God. 2 Corinthians 1:4

▸ Know that I am Always bearing about in the body the dying of the Lord Jesus, that the life also of Jesus might be made manifest in our body. 2 Corinthians 4:10

▸ Know For we which live are alway delivered unto death for Jesus' sake, that the life also of Jesus might be made manifest in our mortal flesh. 2 Corinthians 4:11

MY REACTIONS TO TRIALS SHOULD BE:

REJOICE! Because it shows I identify with Jesus' suffering and I am a partaker in His sufferings. 2 Corinthians 4:13 Shouldn't I want to identify with Jesus?

Watch this.... If I am reproached for the name of Jesus I should be very happy because this declares that the spirit of glory and of God resteth upon me. 2 Corinthians 4:14

POINTS:

Suffering for doing well; the name of Jesus, or as a Christian/Saint is a good type of suffering and my *response to this type of suffering should be*:

1. Glorify God on this behalf 2 Corinthians 4:16
2. Commit the keeping of my soul to God in well doing 2 Corinthians 4:19
3. Because God is a faithful Creator 2 Corinthians 4:19

POINT AND PURPOSE OF SUFFERING:
After....That ye have suffered a while, *make* you perfect, stablished, strengthen, settle you 1 Peter 5:1

POINTS OF PURPOSE FOR TRIALS: 1 Peter 4:12

Don't act like something strange has happened to me because I am going through a fiery trial.... Because the purpose of those trial is to try me: 1 Peter 4:12

▸ Know Jesus said in John 16: 33 These things I have spoken unto you,

▸ that in me ye might have peace.

▸ In the world *ye shall have* tribulation: but be of good cheer; I have overcome the world.

▸ Knowing that tribulation worketh patience Romans 5:13

HOW TO RESPOND TO BEING USED (Luke 6:27-38)

1. Love my enemies

2. Do good to them that hate me

3. Bless them that curse me

4. Pray for them which despitefully use me

5. When hit or things taken; forgive and give more

6. Give, give; when my goods taken just let it go; don't try to get it back

7. Treat people like I want to be treated

8. Be different than the sinner cause they only love, do good, and lend to whom they receive from

9. But I am to love, help, lend not to get again because my reward shall be great!

MY POSITION IN JESUS CHRIST

Strengthened with all might, according to his glorious power, unto all patience and longsuffering with joyfulness Colossians 1:11

As ye have therefore received Christ Jesus the Lord, so walk ye in him: Colossians 2:6

Rooted and built up in him, and stablished in the faith, as ye have been taught, abounding therein with thanksgiving. Colossians 2:7

To whom God would make known what is the riches of the glory of this mystery among the Gentiles; which is Christ in you, the hope of glory: Colossians 1:27

And hath raised us up together and *made* us sit together in heavenly places in Christ Jesus: Ephesians 2:6

In whom we have boldness and access with confidence by the faith of him. Ephesians 3:12

And ye are complete in him, which is the head of all princi-pality and power: Colossians 2:10

For whatsoever is born of God overcometh the world: and

this is the victory that overcometh the world even our faith 1 John 5:4

To the praise of the glory of his grace, wherein he hath *made* us accepted in the beloved Ephesians 1:6

In whom also we have obtained an inheritance Ephesians 1:11

In whom ye also trusted, after that ye heard the word of truth the gospel of your salvation: in whom also after that ye believed, ye were sealed with that holy Spirit of promise. Ephesians 1:13

In whom ye also are builded together for an habitation of God through the Spirit. Ephesians 2:22

Ye are of God, little children, and have overcome them: because greater is he that is in you, than he that is in the world. 1 John 4:4

APPENDIX

MENTAL HEALTH SCRIPTURES

EPHESIANS 1:12-14

That we should be to the praise of his glory, who first trusted in Christ. In whom ye also trusted, after that ye heard the word of truth, the gospel of your salvation: in whom also after that ye believed, ye were sealed with the holy Spirit of promise. Which is the earnest of our inheritance until the redemption of the purchase possession, unto the praise of his glory!

COLOSSIANS 2:6-7

As ye have therefore received Christ Jesus the Lord, so walk in him: rooted and built up in him and stablished in the faith, as ye have been taught, abounding therein with thanksgiving.

COLOSSIANS 1:11

Strengthened with all might, according to his glorious power, unto all patience and longsuffering with joyfulness

2 PETER 1:3

According to his divine power hath given unto us all things that pertain unto life and godliness, through the knowledge of him that hath call us to glory and virtue

2 PETER 1:4

Whereby are given unto us exceeding great and precious promises: that by these ye might be partakers of the divine nature having escaped corruption that is in the world through lust.

ROMANS 8:32

He spared not his own Son, but delivered him up for us all, how shall he not with him also freely give us all things

EPHESIANS 3:20

Now unto him that is able to do *exceeding abundantly* above all that we ask or think, according to the power that worketh in us

PHILIPPIANS 1:6

Being confident of this very thing, that he which hath begun a good work in you will perform it until the day of Jesus Christ.

EPHESIANS 2:6

And hath raised us up together, and *made* us sit together in heavenly places in Christ Jesus!

EPHESIANS 3:12

In whom we have boldness and access with confidence by

the faith of him

COLOSSIANS 2:10

And ye are complete in him, which is the head of all principality and power

HEBREWS 13:5

God says "I will never leave thee nor forsake thee!"

COLOSSIANS 3:3

For you are dead, and your life is *hid* with Christ in God.

ACTS 17:28

For in him we live, and move, and have our being; as certain also of your own poets have said, For we are also his offspring

ROMANS 5:17

For if by one man's offence death reigned by one; much more they which *receive abundance of grace* and of the *gift of righteousness shall reign* in life by one, Jesus Christ.

2 CORINTHIANS 12:9

My grace is sufficient for thee, for my strength is made perfect in weakness

ROMANS 8:1

There is therefore now no condemnation for those who are in Christ Jesus ....

PSALMS 5:12

For thou Lord, wilt bless the righteous, with favor wilt thou compass him as with a shield

ROMANS 8: 2

For the law of the Spirit of Life in Christ Jesus hath made me free from the law of sin and death!

GALATIANS 3:13

Christ hath redeemed us from the curse of the law, being *made* a curse for us: for it is written, Cursed is every one that hangeth on a tree:

JUDE 1:24-25

Now unto him that is able to keep you from falling, and to present *you* faultless before the presence of his glory with exceeding joy.

PSALMS 107:2

Let the redeemed of the Lord say so, whom he hath redeemed from the hand of the enemy!

HEBREWS 10:35

Cast not away therefore your confidence, which hath great recompence of reward.

2 TIMOTHY 1:7

For God hath not given us the spirit of fear; but of power, and of love and of a sound mind.

JOHN 14:27

Peace I leave with you; my peace I give unto you: not as the world giveth, give I unto you. Let not your heart be troubled, neither let it be afraid

ISAIAH 26:3

Thou wilt keep him in perfect peace, whose mind is stayed on thee: because he trusteth in thee.

ROMANS 12:2

Be not conform to this world, but be transformed by the re-newing of your mind. That I may prove what is that good, acceptable and perfect will of God.

ISAIAH 41:10

Fear not, for I am with you; be not dismayed, for I am your God; I will strengthen you, I will help you, yea I will uphold you with the right hand of my righteousness.

PSALMS 16:11
Thou wilt shew me the path of life: in thy presence is the fullness of joy: at thy right hand there are pleasures forevermore.

LAMENTATIONS 3:22-23
It is of the Lord's mercies that we are not consumed, because his compassions fail not. They are new every morning: great is thy faithfulness.

PSALMS 3:3
But thou, O Lord, art a shield for me; my glory, and the lifter up of my head!

COLOSSIANS 1:27
To whom God would make known what *is* the riches of the glory of this mystery among the Gentiles; which is Christ in you the hope of glory.

Also note the riches of his grace!

EPHESIANS 2:7
That in the ages to come he might shew the exceeding riches of his grace in his kindness toward us through Christ Jesus

JAMES 4: 7

Submit yourself to God, Resist the devil and he will flee

EPHESIANS 4:27

Neither Give place to the devil
(Revelation 12:8 devil prevailed not and their place was not found anymore in heaven!)

EPHESIANS 6: 11

Put on the whole armour of God, that ye may be able to stand against the wiles of the devil!

HEBREWS 4:15-16

For we have not an high priest which cannot be touched with the feeling of our infirmities; but was in all points tempted like as we are, yet without sin. Let us therefore come boldly unto the throne of grace, that we may obtain mercy, and find grace to help in time of need.

PSALMS 121:1-2

I will lift up my eyes unto the hills, from whence cometh my help. My help cometh from the Lord, which made heaven and earth.

V.5 The Lord is my keeper
V.7 The Lord shall preserve me from all evil

V.8 The Lord shall preserve my going out and my coming in.

PSALMS 46:1-3

God is our refuge and strength, a very present help in the time of trouble. Therefore we will not fear.

JEREMIAH 29:11

For I know the thoughts that I think toward you, saith the Lord, thoughts of peace, and not of evil, to give you an expected end For surely I know the plans I have for you, says the Lord, plans for your welfare and not for harm, to give you a future with hope!

1 JOHN 5:4

For whatsoever is born of God overcometh the world: and this is the victory that overcometh the world, even our faith

PHILIPPIANS 3:13, 14

But this one thing I do: forgetting those things which are behind and reaching forth unto those things which are before, I press toward the mark for the prize of the high calling of God in Christ Jesus.

PHILIPPIANS 4:8A

Finally, brethren, whatsoever things are true, whatsoever

things are honest, whatsoever things are just, whatsoever things are pure, whatsoever things are lovely, whatsoever things are of good reports; if there be any virtue, and if there be any praise, think on these things.

ROMANS 8:28

And we know that all things work together for good to them that love God, to them who are the called according to his purpose.

JOSHUA 1:9

Have I not commanded thee? Be strong and of good courage. Be not afraid, neither be thou dismayed: for the Lord thy God is with me whithersoever I goest.

PHILIPPIANS 4:13

I can do all things through Christ who strengthens me

PSALMS 34:17-20

When the righteous cry for help, and the Lord heareth and delivereth them out of all their troubles. The Lord is nigh unto them that are of a broken heart and saveth such as be of a contrite spirit. Many are the afflictions of the righteous, but the Lord delivereth him out of them all. He keepeth all his bones; not one of them is broken.

1 CORINTHIANS 10:13

There hath no temptation taken you but such as is common to man. But God is faithful, who will not suffer you to be tempted above that you are able, but will with the temptation also make a way to escape, that you may be able to bear it.

PHILIPPIANS 4:6-7

Be careful for nothing; but in everything by prayer and supplication with thanksgiving let your requests be made known to God. And the peace of God, which surpasseth all understanding, shall keep your hearts and minds through Christ Jesus.

PHILIPPIANS 4:19

But my God shall supply all your need according to his riches in glory by Christ Jesus.

PSALMS 56:11

In God have I put my trust; I will not be afraid what can man do unto me?

LUKE 1:37

For with God nothing shall be impossible with God.

JOHN 15:7

If you abide in me and my words abide in you, ye shall ask what ye will, and it shall be done unto you!

POWER OF MADE USED IN SCRIPTURES

ROMANS 5:19

For as by one man's disobedience many were made sinners, so by the obedience of one shall many be made righteous.

ROMANS 6:18

Being then made free from sin, ye became the servants of righteousness.

ROMANS 6:22

But now being made free from sin, and become servants to God, ye have your fruit unto holiness, and the end everlasting life.

ROMANS 2:8

For the law of the Spirit of life in Christ Jesus hath made me free from the law of sin and death.

GALATIANS 5:1

Stand fast therefore in the liberty wherewith Christ hath made us free, and be not entangled again with the yoke of bondage

ROMANS 10:10

For with the heart man believeth unto righteousness; and with the mouth confession is made unto salvation.

1 CORINTHIANS 15:22

For as in Adam all die, even so in Christ shall all be made alive.

2 CORINTHIANS 4:10

Always bearing about in the body the dying of the Lord Jesus, that the life also of Jesus might be made manifest in our body.

2 CORINTHIANS 4:11

For we which live are alway delivered unto death for Jesus' sake, that the life also of Jesus might be made manifest in our mortal flesh.

2 CORINTHIANS 4:21

For he hath made him to be sin for us, who knew no sin; that we might be made the righteousness of God in him.

2 CORINTHIANS 12:9

And he said unto me, My grace is sufficient for thee: for my strength is made perfect in weakness. Most gladly therefore will I rather glory in my infirmities, that the power of Christ may rest upon me.

GALATIANS 3:13

Christ hath redeemed us from the curse of the law, being made a curse for us: for it is written, Cursed is every one that hangeth on a tree:

EPHESIANS 2:6

And hath raised us up together, and made us sit together in heavenly places in Christ Jesus:

EPHESIANS 2:13

But now in Christ Jesus ye who sometimes were far off are made nigh by the blood of Christ.

EPHESIANS 2:14

For he is our peace, who hath made both one, and hath broken down the middle wall of partition between us;

COLOSSIANS 1:20

And, having made peace through the blood of his cross, by him to reconcile all things unto himself; by him, I say, whether they be things in earth, or things in heaven.

COLOSSIANS 2:15

And having spoiled principalities and powers, he made a

shew of them openly, triumphing over them in it.

TITUS 3:7

That being justified by his grace, we should be made heirs according to the hope of eternal life.

HEBREWS 3:17

For we are made partakers of Christ, if we hold the beginning of our confidence steadfast unto the end;

HOW JESUS MADE

MARK 6:56

And whithersoever he entered, into villages, or cities, or country, they laid the sick in the streets, and besought him that they might touch if it were but the border of his garment: and as many as touched him were made whole.

MARK 10:52

And Jesus said unto him, Go thy way; thy faith hath made thee whole. And immediately he received his sight, and followed Jesus in the way.

LUKE 8:48

And he said unto her, Daughter, be of good comfort: thy faith hath made thee whole; go in peace.

LUKE 8:50

But when Jesus heard it, he answered him, saying, Fear not: believe only, and she shall be made whole.

LUKE 13:13

And he laid his hands on her: and immediately she was made straight, and glorified God.

JOHN 1:3

All things were made by him; and without him was not anything made that was made.

JOHN 1:10

He was in the world, and the world was made by him, and the world knew him not.

JOHN 1:14

And the Word was made flesh, and dwelt among us, (and we beheld his glory, the glory as of the only begotten of the Father,) full of grace and truth

JOHN 5:4

For an angel went down at a certain season into the pool, and troubled the water: whosoever then first after the troubling of the water stepped in was made whole of whatsoever disease he had.

JOHN 5:6

When Jesus saw him lie, and knew that he had been now a long time in that case, he saith unto him, Wilt thou be made whole?

JOHN 5:9

And immediately the man was made whole, and took up his bed, and walked: and on the same day was the sabbath.

JOHN 5:11

He answered them, He that made me whole, the same said unto me, Take up thy bed, and walk.

JOHN 5:14

Afterward Jesus findeth him in the temple, and said unto him, Behold, thou art made whole: sin no more, lest a worse thing come unto thee.

1 JOHN 4:17

Herein is our love made perfect, that we may have boldness in the day of judgment: because as he is, so are we in this world.

1 JOHN 4:18

There is no fear in love; but perfect love casteth out fear:

because fear hath torment. He that feareth is not made perfect in love.

REVELATION 1:6

And hath made us kings and priests unto God and his Father; to him be glory and dominion for ever and ever. Amen.

WHAT TO PUT ON

ROMANS 13:12

The night is far spent, the day is at hand: let us therefore cast off the works of darkness, and let us put on the armour of light.

1 CORINTHIANS 15:53

For this corruptible must put on incorruption, and this mortal must put on immortality.

1 CORINTHIANS 15:54

So when this corruptible shall have put on incorruption, and this mortal shall have put on immortality, then shall be brought to pass the saying that is written, Death is swallowed up in victory.

GALATIANS 3:27

For as many of you as have been baptized into Christ have put on Christ.

EPHESIANS 4:24

And that ye put on the new man, which after God is created in righteousness and true holiness.

EPHESIANS 6:11

Put on the whole armour of God, that ye may be able to stand against the wiles of the devil.

COLOSSIANS 3:10

And have put on the new man, which is renewed in knowledge after the image of him that created him:

COLOSSIANS 3:12

Put on therefore, as the elect of God, holy and beloved, bowels of mercies, kindness, humbleness of mind, meekness, longsuffering;

COLOSSIANS 3:14

And above all these things put on charity, which is the bond of perfectness.

SUMMARY OF WHAT TO PUT ON:

1. Armor of light
2. Incorruption
3. Immortality
4. Put on Jesus
5. New man created in righteousness and true holiness

6. Whole armor of God

7. New man renewed in knowledge

8. Bowels of mercies, kindness,

9. Humbleness of mind, meekness,

10. Long suffering and charity

THE PROUD

This is why there is a problem with being proud look at the results it brings.

PROVERBS 28:25

He that is of a proud heart stirreth up strife: but he that putteth his trust in the Lord shall be made fat.

1 TIMOTHY 6:3

If any man teach otherwise, and *consent not to wholesome words, even the words of our Lord Jesus Christ, and to the doctrine which is according to godliness;*

V.4 He is proud, knowing nothing, but doting about questions and strifes of words, whereof cometh envy, strife, railings, evil surmisings,

V.5 Perverse disputings of men of corrupt minds, and destitute of the truth, supposing that gain is godliness: from such withdraw thyself.

V.6 But godliness with contentment is great gain.

PROVERBS 29:22

An angry man stirreth up strife, and a furious man aboundeth in transgression.

PROVERBS 21:4

An high look, and a proud heart, and the plowing of the wicked, is sin.

JAMES 3:16

For where envying and strife is, there is confusion and every evil work.

HOW GOD INTERACTS WITH THE PROUD:

PSALMS 119:21

Thou hast rebuked the proud that are cursed, which do err from thy commandments.

PROVERBS 6:16

These six things doth the Lord hate: yea, seven are an abomination unto him:

PROVERBS 6:17

A proud look, a lying tongue, and hands that shed innocent blood,

PROVERBS 6:18

An heart that deviseth wicked imaginations, feet that be swift in running to mischief,

PROVERBS 6:19

A false witness that speaketh lies, and he that soweth discord among brethren.

PROVERBS 15:25

The Lord will *destroy* the house of the proud: but he will establish the border of the widow.

PROVERBS 16:5

Every one that is proud in heart is *an abomination* to the Lord: though hand join in hand, he shall not be unpunished.

ISAIAH 2:12

For the day of the LORD of hosts shall be upon every one that is proud and lofty, and upon every one that is lifted up; and he *shall be brought low:*

JEREMIAH 50:31

Behold, *I am against thee*, O thou most proud, saith the Lord God of hosts: for thy day is come, the time that I will visit thee.

V.32 And the most proud shall stumble and fall, and none shall raise him up: and I will kindle a fire in his cities, and it shall devour all round about him.

LUKE 1:51

He hath shewed strength with his arm; *he hath scattered* the proud in the imagination of their hearts.

JAMES 4:6

But he giveth more grace. Wherefore he saith, God resisteth the proud, but giveth grace unto the humble.

1 PETER 5:5

Likewise, ye younger, submit yourselves unto the elder. Yea, all of you be subject one to another, and be clothed with humility: for God *resisteth* the proud, and giveth grace to the humble.

Summary of God's reaction to the proud

Rebukes, hates, destroys, an abomination, brought low, scattered, resist, against, devour (stumble, fall).

WHAT MY RESPONSE TO BEING PROUD SHOULD BE

PSALMS 119:78

Let the proud *be ashamed*; for they dealt perversely with me without a cause: but I will *meditate in thy precepts.*

PROVERBS 16:19

Better it is to be of *an humble spirit with the lowly*, than to divide the spoil with the proud.

1 PETER 5:5

Likewise, ye younger, submit yourselves unto the elder. Yea, all of you be subject one to another, and be clothed with humility: for *God resisteth the proud*, and giveth grace to the humble.

1 PETER 5:6

Humble yourselves therefore under the mighty hand of God, that he may exalt you in due time:

1 PETER 5:7

Casting all your care upon him; for he careth for you.

1 PETER 5:8

Be vigilant; because your adversary the devil, as a roaring lion, walketh about, seeking whom he may devour:

1 PETER 5:9

Whom resist stedfast in the faith, knowing that the same afflictions are accomplished in your brethren that are in the world.

TYPES OF CONSCIENCES

GOOD CONSCIENCE

ACTS: 23:1

And Paul, earnestly beholding the council, said, Men and brethren, I have lived in all good conscience before God until this day.

1 TIMOTHY 1:15

Now the end of the commandment is charity out of a pure heart, and of a good conscience, and of faith unfeigned:

HEBREWS 13:18

Pray for us: for we trust we have a good conscience, in all things willing to live honestly.

1 TIMOTHY 1:19

Holding faith, and a good conscience; which some having put away concerning faith have made shipwreck:

1 PETER 3:6

Having a good conscience; that, whereas they speak evil of you, as of evildoers, they may be ashamed that falsely accuse your good conversation in Christ.

1 PETER 3:21

The like figure whereunto even baptism doth also now save us not the putting away of the filth of the flesh, but the answer of a good conscience toward God, by the resurrection of Jesus Christ:

VOICE OF OFFENCE

ACTS 24:16

And herein do I exercise myself, to have always a conscience void of offence toward God, and toward men.

PURE CONSCIENCE

1 TIMOTHY 3:19

Holding the mystery of the faith in a pure conscience.

2 TIMOTHY 1:3

I thank God, whom I serve from my forefathers with pure conscience, that without ceasing I have remembrance of thee in my prayers night and day;

PROTECTING OUR CONSCIENCE

ROMANS 13:5

Wherefore ye must needs be subject, not only for wrath, but also for conscience sake.

2 CORINTHIANS 2:4

But have renounced the hidden things of dishonesty, not walking in craftiness, nor handling the word of God deceitfully; but by manifestation of the truth commending ourselves to every man's conscience in the sight of God.

TITUS 1:15

Unto the pure all things are pure: but unto them that are defiled and unbelieving is nothing pure; but even their mind and conscience is defiled.

1 PETER 2:19

For this is thankworthy, if a man for conscience toward God endure grief, suffering wrongfully.

Problem: weak conscience encourages weakness

1 CORINTHIANS 8:7

Howbeit there is not in every man that knowledge: for some with conscience of the idol unto this hour eat it as a thing offered unto an idol; and their conscience being weak is defiled.

1 CORINTHIANS 8:10

For if any man see thee which hast knowledge sit at meat in the idol's temple, shall not the conscience of him which is weak be emboldened to eat those things which are offered to idols;

WOUNDING CONSCIENCES

1 CORINTHIANS 8:12

But when ye sin so against the brethren, and wound their weak conscience, ye sin against Christ.

TYPE OF CONSCIENCE TO DISPLAY WHEN EATING

1 CORINTHIANS 10:27

If any of them that believe not bid you to a feast, and ye be disposed to go; whatsoever is set before you, eat, asking no question for conscience sake.

1 CORINTHIANS 10:25

Whatsoever is sold in the shambles, that eat, asking no question for conscience sake:

1 CORINTHIANS 10:28

But if any man say unto you, This is offered in sacrifice unto idols, eat not for his sake that shewed it, and for conscience sake: for the earth is the Lord's, and the fulness thereof:

CONSCIENCE PURGED WITH THE BLOOD OF JESUS

HEBREWS 9:14

How much more shall the blood of Christ, who through the eternal Spirit offered himself without spot to God, purge your conscience from dead works to serve the living God?

HEBREWS 9:9

Which was a figure for the time then present, in which were offered both gifts and sacrifices, that could not make him that did the service perfect, as pertaining to the conscience;

HEBREWS 10: 2

For then would they have ceased to be offered? Because that the worshippers once purged should have had no more conscience of sins

HEBREWS 10: 22

Let us draw near with a true heart in full assurance of faith, having our hearts sprinkled from an evil conscience, and our bodies washed with pure water.

CONVICTED CONSCIENCE

JOHN 8:9

And they which heard it, being convicted by their own conscience, went out one by one, beginning at the eldest, even unto the last: and Jesus was left alone, and the woman standing in the midst.

SEARED CONSCIENCE

1TIMOTHY 4:2

Speaking lies in hypocrisy; having their conscience seared with a hot iron;

GOD'S POSITION ON ANGER

NEHEMIAH 9:17 but thou art a God ready to pardon, gracious and merciful, slow to anger, and of great kindness, and forsookest them not

PSALMS 30:5 For his anger endureth but a moment; in his favour is life: weeping may endure for a night, but joy cometh in the morning.

PSALMS 145:8-9 The Lord is gracious, and full of compassion; slow to anger, and of great mercy.

JESUS' TAKE ON ANGER

MARK 3:1-2 And when he had looked round about on them with anger, being grieved for the hardness of their hearts, he saith unto the man, Stretch forth thine hand. And he stretched it out: and his hand was restored whole as the other.

MATTHEW 21:12-14 And Jesus went into the temple of God, and cast out all them that sold and bought in the temple, and overthrew the tables of the moneychangers, and the seats of them that sold doves,

MATTHEW 21:13 And said unto them, It is written, My

house shall be called the house of prayer; but ye have made it a den of thieves.

EFFECTS OF UNJUSTIFIED ANGER

MATTHEW 5:22 But I say unto you, That whosoever is angry with his brother without a cause shall be in danger of the judgment: and whosoever shall say to his brother, Raca, shall be in danger of the council: but whosoever shall say, Thou fool, shall be in danger of hell fire.

WHAT MY RESPONSES AND STANCES SHOULD BE ABOUT ANGER

PSALMS 37:8 Cease from anger, and forsake wrath: fret not thyself in any wise to do evil.

PROVERBS 15:1 A soft answer turneth away wrath: but grievous words stir up anger.

PROVERBS 15:18 A wrathful man stirreth up strife: but he that is slow to anger *appeaseth strife.*

PROVERBS 16:32 He that is slow to anger is better than the mighty; and he that ruleth his spirit than he that taketh a city.

PROVERBS 17:14 The beginning of strife is as when one

letteth out water: therefore leave off contention, before it be meddled with.

PROVERBS 19:11 The discretion of a man deferreth his anger; and it is his glory to pass over a transgression.

COLOSSIANS 3:21 Fathers, provoke not your children to anger, lest they be discouraged.

PROVERBS 21:19 The discretion of a man deferreth his anger; and it is his glory to pass over a transgression.

PROVERBS 27:4 Wrath is cruel, and anger is outrageous; but who is able to stand before envy?

ECCLESIASTES 7:9 Be not hasty in thy spirit to be angry: for anger resteth in the bosom of fools.

ROMANS 12:19 Dearly beloved, avenge not yourselves, but rather give place unto wrath: for it is written, vengeance is mine; I will repay, saith the Lord

ROMANS 12:20 Therefore if thine enemy hunger, feed him; if he thirst, give him drink: for in so doing thou shalt heap coals of fire on his head

ROMANS 12:21 Be not overcome of evil, but overcome evil

with good.

COLOSSIANS 3:7-9 But now ye also put off all these; anger, wrath, malice, blasphemy, filthy communication out of your mouth.

PROVERBS 20:3 It is an honour for a man to cease from strife: but every fool will be meddling.

EPHESIANS 4:26 Be ye angry, and sin not: let not the sun go down upon your wrath:

EPHESIANS 4: 27 Neither give place to the devil.

EPHESIANS 4:31 Let all bitterness, and wrath, and anger, and clamour, and evil speaking, be put away from you, with all malice

JAMES 1:17 Wherefore, my beloved brethren, let every man be swift to hear, slow to speak, slow to wrath:

DANGERS AND DESTRUCTION OF ANGER

2 TIMOTHY 2:23-24 But foolish and unlearned questions avoid, knowing that they do gender strifes.

PROVERBS 29:22 An angry man stirreth up strife, and a furious man aboundeth in transgression.

PROVERBS 22:24-25 Make no friendship with an angry man; and with a furious man thou shalt not go:

PROVERBS 30:33 Surely the churning of milk bringeth forth butter, and the wringing of the nose bringeth forth blood: so the forcing of wrath bringeth forth strife

PROVERBS 14:17 He that is soon angry dealeth foolishly: and a man of wicked devices is hated.

PRAYER

Note: God deems our prayers as being so precious, so valuable, that he requires them to be collected by angels and stored in golden vials!

REVELATION 5:8 And when he had taken the book, the four beasts and four and twenty elders fell down before the Lamb, having every one of them harps, and golden vials full of odours, which are the prayers of saints.

REVELATION 8:3 And another angel came and stood at the altar, having a golden censer; and there was given unto him much incense, that he should offer it with the prayers of all saints upon the golden altar which was before the throne.

V.4 And the smoke of the incense, which came with the prayers of the saints, ascended up before God out of the angel's hand

JOB 22:28 Thou shalt also decree a thing, and it shall be established unto thee: and the light shall shine upon thy ways.

PSALMS 65:2 O thou that hearest prayer, unto thee shall all flesh come.

109

JESUS LIVETH TO MAKE INTERCESSION FOR US NOW DAILY - THE HOLY GHOST MAKES INTERCESSION FOR US

HEBREW 7:25 Wherefore he is able also to save them to the uttermost that come unto God by him, seeing he ever liveth to make intercession for them.

ROMANS 8:26 Likewise the Spirit also helpeth our infirmities: for we know not what we should pray for as we ought: but the Spirit itself maketh intercession for us with groanings which cannot be uttered.

V.27 And he that searcheth the hearts knoweth what is the mind of the Spirit, because he maketh intercession for the saints according to the will of God.

ROMANS 8:34 Who is he that condemneth? It is Christ that died, yea rather, that is risen again, who is even at the right hand of God, who also maketh intercession for us.

JESUS PRAYING MORE THAN ONCE

MATTHEW 26:42 He went away again the second time, and prayed, saying, O my Father, if this cup may not pass away from me, except I drink it, thy will be done.

V.44 And he left them, and went away again, and prayed the third time, saying the same words.

MARK 14:35 And he went forward a little, and fell on the ground, and prayed that, if it were possible, the hour might pass from him.

V.39 And again he went away, and prayed, and spake the same words.

LUKE 22:41 And he was withdrawn from them about a stone's cast, and kneeled down, and prayed,

V.44 And being in an agony he prayed more earnestly: and his sweat was as it were great drops of blood falling down to the ground.

LUKE 3:21 Now when all the people were baptized, it came to pass, that Jesus also being baptized, and praying, the heaven was opened

JAMES 5:17 Elias was a man subject to like passions as we are, and he prayed earnestly that it might not rain: and it rained not on the earth by the space of three years and six months.

V.18 And he prayed again, and the heaven gave rain, and the earth brought forth her fruit.

JESUS' SOLITARY PRAYER & ALL NIGHT PRAYER

MARK 1:35 And in the morning, rising up a great while before day, he went out, and departed into a solitary place, and there prayed.

LUKE 5:16 And he withdrew himself into the wilderness, and prayed.

LUKE 6:11 And they were filled with madness; and communed one with another what they might do to Jesus.

V.12 And it came to pass in those days, that he went out into a mountain to pray, and continued all night in prayer to God.

LUKE 8:28 And it came to pass about an eight days after these sayings, he took Peter and John and James, and went up into a mountain to pray.

V.9 And as he prayed, the fashion of his countenance was altered, and his raiment was white and glistering.

112

PRAYING IN THE HOLY GHOST

JUDE 1:20 But ye, beloved, building up yourselves on your most holy faith, praying in the Holy Ghost

GOD REVEALS DURING PRAYER

DANIEL 9:21 Yea, whiles I was speaking in prayer, even the man Gabriel, whom I had seen in the vision at the beginning, being caused to fly swiftly, touched me about the time of the evening oblation.

V.22 And he informed me, and talked with me, and said, O Daniel, I am now come forth to give thee skill and understanding.

PRAYER TO REVEAL

2 KINGS 6:17 And Elisha prayed, and said, Lord, I pray thee, open his eyes, that he may see. And the Lord opened the eyes of the young man; and he saw: and, behold, the mountain was full of horses and chariots of fire round about Elisha.

V.18 And when they came down to him, Elisha prayed unto the Lord, and said, Smite this people, I pray thee, with blindness. And he smote them with blindness according to the word of Elisha.

PRAYING FOR OTHERS BRINGS OUR DELIVERANCES

JOB 42:10 And the Lord turned the captivity of Job, when he prayed for his friends: also the Lord gave Job twice as much as he had before

PRAYER FOR AND LAYING HANDS ON THE SICK

ACTS 28:8 And it came to pass, that the father of Publius lay sick of a fever and of a bloody flux: to whom Paul entered in, and prayed, and laid his hands on him, and healed him.

JAMES 5:14 Is any sick among you? let him call for the elders of the church; and let them pray over him, anointing him with oil in the name of the Lord:

V.15 And the prayer of faith shall save the sick, and the Lord shall raise him up; and if he have committed sins, they shall be forgiven him.

POWER IN PRAYER

ACTS 4:31 And when they had prayed, the place was shaken where they were assembled together; and they were all filled with the Holy Ghost, and they spake the word of God with boldness.

2 CHRONICLES 7:1 Now when Solomon had made an end of praying, the fire came down from heaven, and consumed the burnt offering and the sacrifices; and the glory of the Lord filled the house.

POSITIONS TO PRAY IN

MATTHEW 26:39 And he (Jesus) went a little farther, and fell on his face, and prayed, saying, O my Father, if it be possible, let this cup pass from me: nevertheless not as I will, but as thou wilt.

ACTS 9:40 But Peter put them all forth, and kneeled down, and prayed; and turning him to the body said, Tabitha, arise. And she opened her eyes: and when she saw Peter, she sat up.

MARK 11:25 And when ye stand praying, forgive, if ye have ought against any: that your Father also which is in heaven may forgive you your trespasses.

1 SAMUEL 1:26 And she said, Oh my lord, as thy soul liveth, my lord, I am the woman that stood by thee here, praying unto the Lord.

2 SAMUEL 7:18 Then went king David in, and sat before the lord, and he said, Who am I, O Lord God? and what is my house, that thou hast brought me hitherto

1 KINGS 8:54 And it was so, that when Solomon had made an end of praying all this prayer and supplication unto the Lord, he arose from before the altar of the Lord, from kneeling on his knees with his hands spread up to heaven.

GOD RESPONDS AND WANTS HIS PEOPLE TO PRAY

1 KINGS 9:3 And the Lord said unto him, I have heard thy prayer and thy supplication, that thou hast made before me: I have hallowed this house, which thou hast built, to put my name there for ever; and mine eyes and mine heart shall be there perpetually.

KINGS 20:5 Turn again, and tell Hezekiah the captain of my people, Thus saith the Lord, the God of David thy father, I have heard thy prayer, I have seen thy tears: behold, I will heal thee: on the third day thou shalt go up unto the house of the Lord

2 CHRONICLES 7:12 And the Lord appeared to Solomon by night, and said unto him, I have heard thy prayer, and have chosen this place to myself for an house of sacrifice.

V.13 If I shut up heaven that there be no rain, or if I command the locusts to devour the land, or if I send pestilence among my people;

V.14 If my people, which are called by my name, shall humble themselves, and pray, and seek my face, and turn from their wicked ways; then will I hear from heaven, and will forgive their sin, and will heal their land.

PSALMS 6:9 The LORD hath heard my supplication; the Lord will receive my prayer.

ISAIAH 38:5 Go, and say to Hezekiah, Thus saith the Lord, the God of David thy father, I have heard thy Prayer, I have seen thy tears: behold, I will add unto thy days fifteen years.

KEEP PRAYER GOING ALL THE TIME

EPHESIANS 6:18 Praying always with all prayer and supplication in the Spirit, and watching thereunto with all perseverance and supplication for all saints

PHILIPPIANS 4:6 Be careful for nothing; but in every thing by prayer and supplication with thanksgiving let your requests be made known unto God.

COLOSSIANS 4:2 Continue in prayer, and watch in the same with thanksgiving;

V.3 Withal praying also for us, that God would open unto us a door of utterance, to speak the mystery of Christ, for which I am also in bonds:

1 PETER 4:7 But the end of all things is at hand: be ye therefore sober, and watch unto prayer

ROMANS 12:12 Rejoicing in hope; patient in tribulation; continuing instant in prayer

PRAYER IS EFFECTIVE

JAMES 5:16 Confess your faults one to another, and pray one for another, that ye may be healed. The effectual fervent prayer of a righteous man availeth much.

V.17 Elias was a man subject to like passions as we are, and he prayed earnestly that it might not rain: and it rained not on the earth by the space of three years and six months.

TIMES OF PRAYER

ACTS 16:25 And at midnight Paul and Silas prayed, and

sang praises unto God: and the prisoners heard them.

PSALMS 5:3 My voice shalt thou hear in the morning, O Lord; in the morning will I direct my prayer unto thee, and will look up.

LUKE 6:12 And it came to pass in those days, that he went out into a mountain to pray, and continued all night in prayer to God.

DANIEL 6:10 Now when Daniel knew that the writing was signed, he went into his house; and his windows being open in his chamber toward Jerusalem, he kneeled upon his knees three times a day, and prayed, and gave thanks before his God, as he did aforetime.

HOUSE OF PRAYER

ISAIAH 56:7 Even them will I bring to my holy mountain, and make them joyful in my house of prayer: their burnt offerings and their sacrifices shall be accepted upon mine altar; for mine house shall be called an house of prayer for all people

MATTHEW 21:13 called the house of prayer; but ye have made it a den of thieves

MARK 11:17 And he taught, saying unto them, Is it not written, My house shall be called of all nations the house of prayer? but ye have made it a den of thieves.

LUKE 19:46 Saying unto them, It is written, My house is the house of prayer: but ye have made it a den of thieves.

CORPORATE & UNIFIED PRAYER

ACTS 12:5 Peter therefore was kept in prison: but prayer was made without ceasing of the church unto God for him.

2 CORINTHIANS 1:9 But we had the sentence of death in ourselves, that we should not trust in ourselves, but in God which raiseth the dead:

V.10 Who delivered us from so great a death, and doth deliver: in whom we trust that he will yet deliver us;

V.11 Ye also helping together by prayer for us, that for the gift bestowed upon us by the means of many persons thanks may be given by many on our behalf.

ACTS 1:14 These all continued with one accord in prayer and supplication, with the women, and Mary the mother of Jesus, and with his brethren

FASTING AND PRAYER

DANIEL 9:3 And I set my face unto the Lord God, to seek by prayer and supplications, with fasting, and sackcloth, and ashes:

MATTHEW 17:20 And Jesus said unto them, Because of your unbelief: for verily I say unto you, If ye have faith as a grain of mustard seed, ye shall say unto this mountain, Remove hence to yonder place and it shall remove; and nothing shall be impossible unto you.

V.21 Howbeit this kind goeth not out but by prayer and fasting.

MARK 9:28 And when he was come into the house, his disciples asked him privately, Why could not we cast him out?

V.29 And he said unto them, This kind can come forth by nothing, but by prayer and fasting.

PRAYER AGAINST CONSPIRACY AND HINDRANCES

NEHEMIAH 4:8 And conspired all of them together to come and to fight against Jerusalem, and to hinder it.

V.9 Nevertheless we made our prayer unto our God, and set a watch against them day and night, because of them.

PRAYER OVER FOOD

1 TIMOTHY 4:5 For it is sanctified by the word of God and prayer. For every creature of God is good, and nothing to be refused, if it be received with thanksgiving:

V.6 If thou put the brethren in remembrance of these things, thou shalt be a good minister of Jesus Christ